UKULELE TRANSCRIPTIONS

JAKE SHIMABUKURO TRIO

JAKE SHIMABUKURO/NOLAN VERNER/DAVE PRESTON

Music transcriptions by Pete Billmann

ISBN 978-1-5400-6356-4

Hal•Leonard®

Visit Hal Leonard Online at
www.halleonard.com

Contact us:
Hal Leonard
7777 West Bluemound Road
Milwaukee, WI 53213
Email: info@halleonard.com

In Europe, contact:
Hal Leonard Europe Limited
42 Wigmore Street
Marylebone, London, W1U 2RN
Email: info@halleonardeurope.com

In Australia, contact:
Hal Leonard Australia Pty. Ltd.
4 Lentara Court
Cheltenham, Victoria, 3192 Australia
Email: info@halleonard.com.au

CONTENTS

When the Masks Come Down

Written by Jake Shimabukuro, Nolan Verner and David Preston Amidei

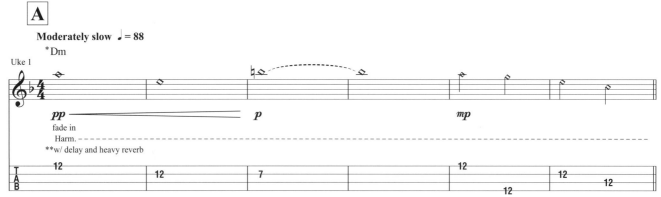

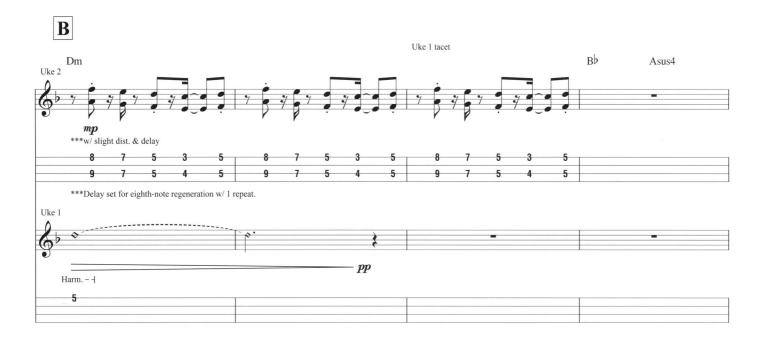

*Chord symbols reflect overall harmony.

**Delay set for eighth-note regeneration w/ 3 repeats.

***Delay set for eighth-note regeneration w/ 1 repeat.

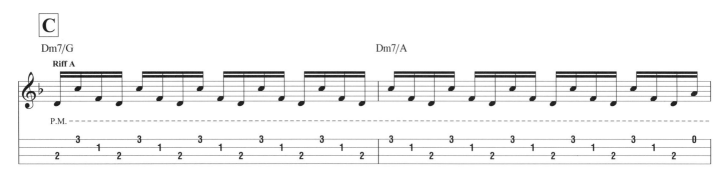

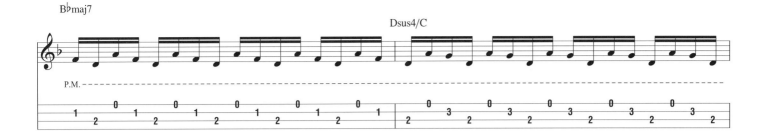

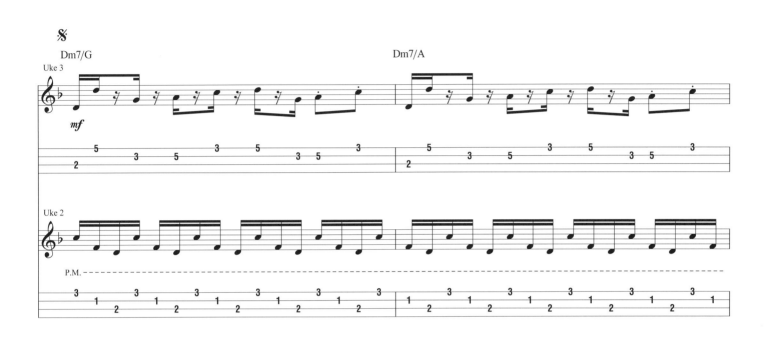

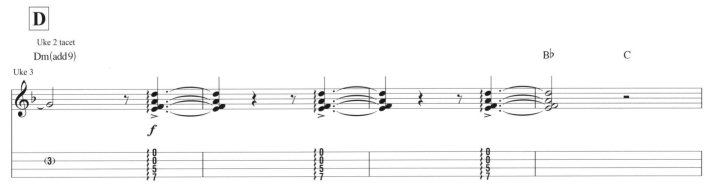

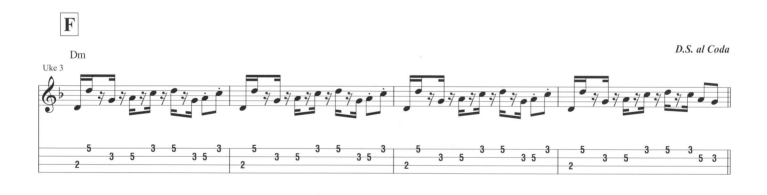

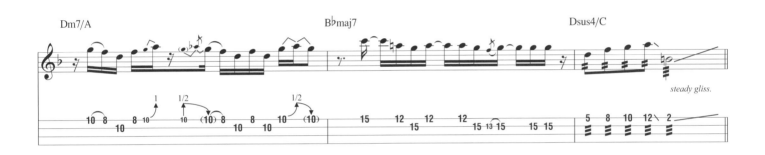

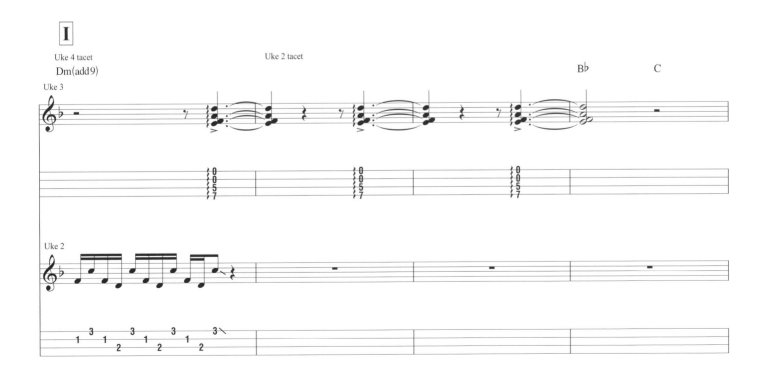

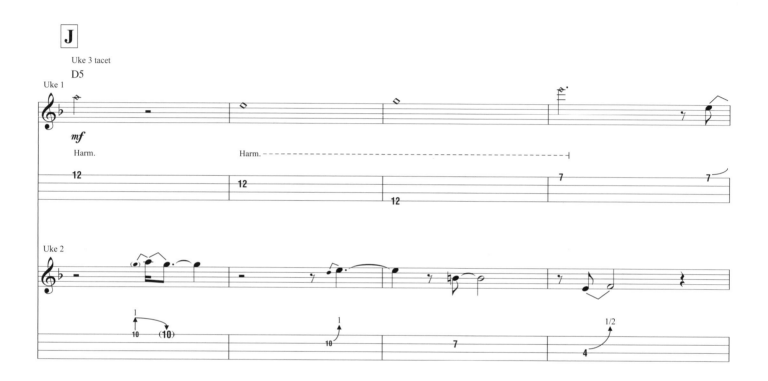

Twelve

Written by Jake Shimabukuro, Nolan Verner and David Preston Amidei

*Chord symbols reflect implied harmony.

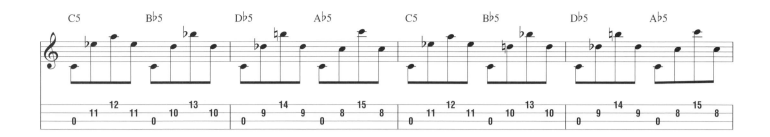

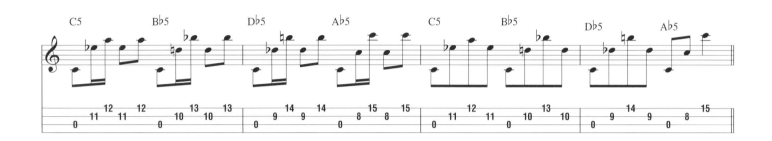

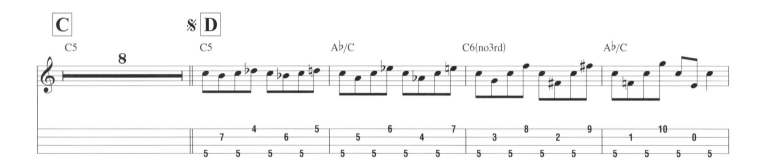

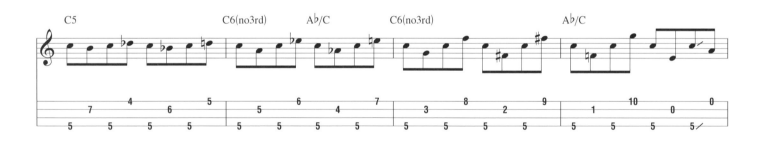

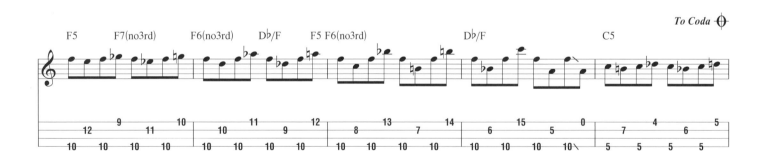

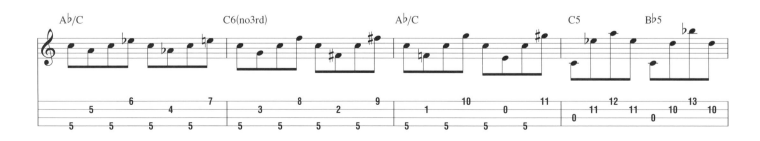

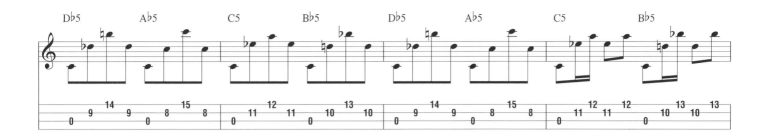

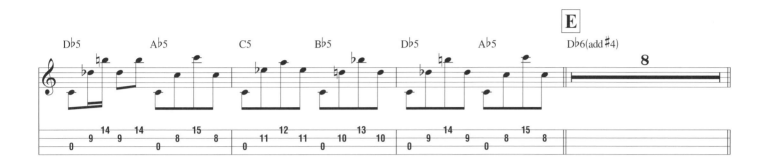

D.S. al Coda

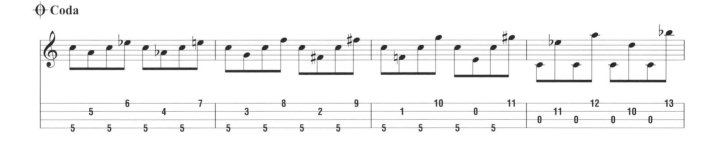

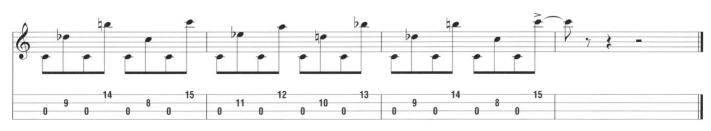

Resistance

Written by Jake Shimabukuro, Nolan Verner and David Preston Amidei

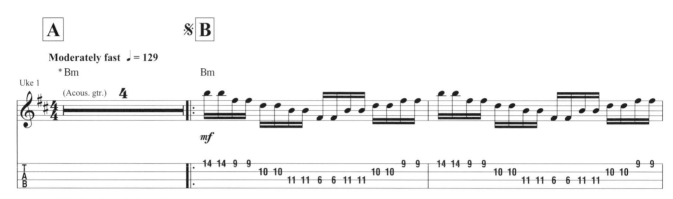

*Chord symbols reflect overall harmony.

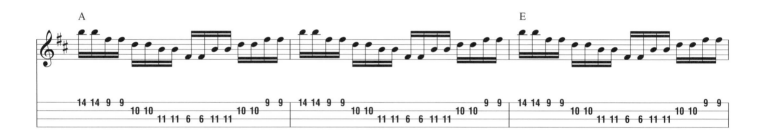

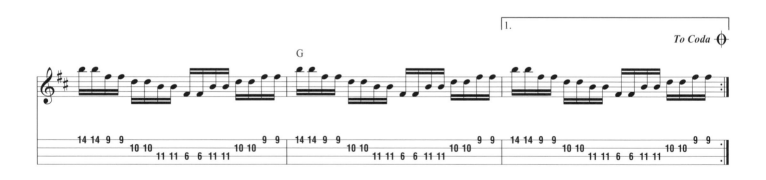

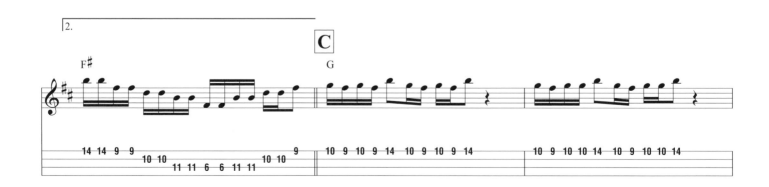

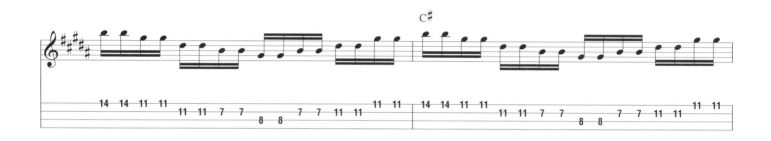

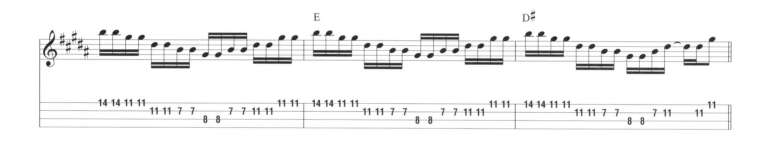

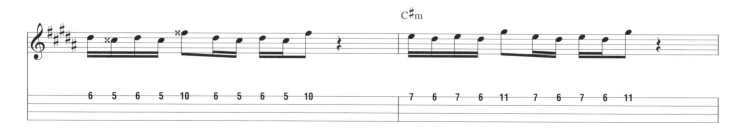

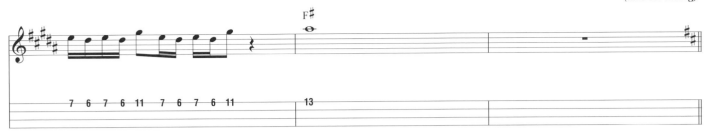

Coda

*Played behind the beat.

H

Half-time feel

Free time
Begin fade   *Fade out*

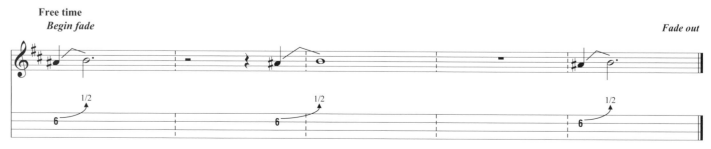

Lament

Written by Jake Shimabukuro, Nolan Verner and David Preston Amidei

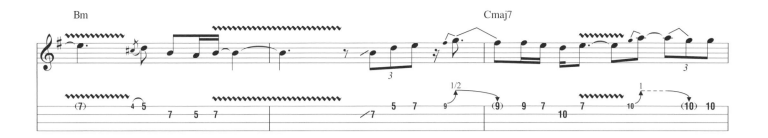

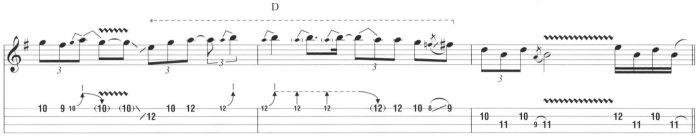

*Played behind the beat.

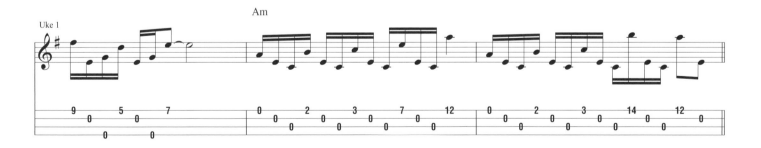

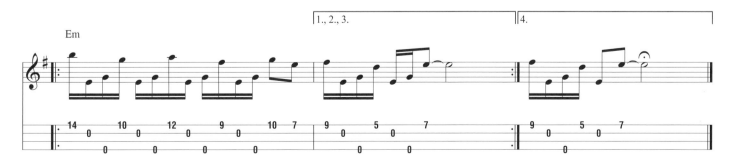

Red Crystal

Written by Jake Shimabukuro, Nolan Verner and David Preston Amidei

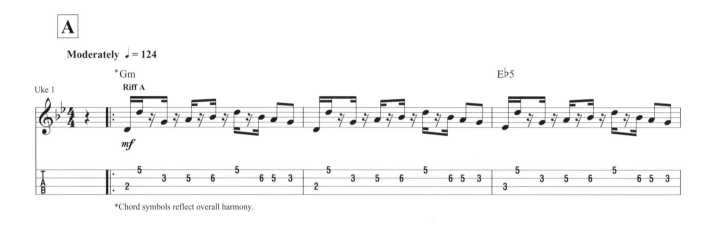

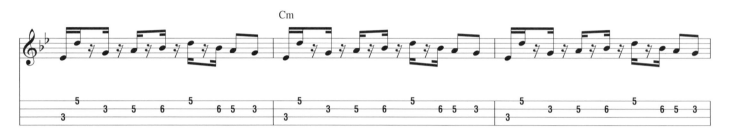

*Chord symbols reflect overall harmony.

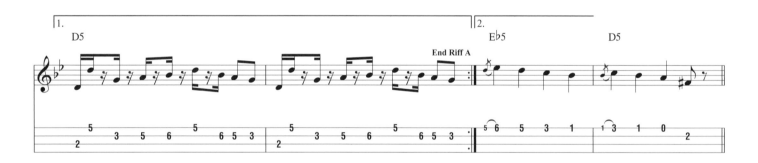

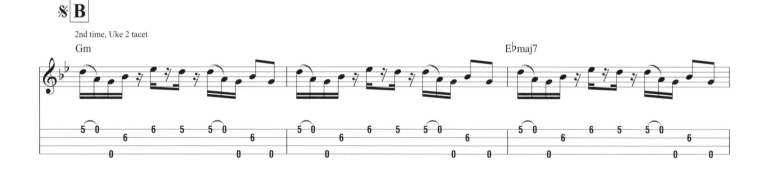

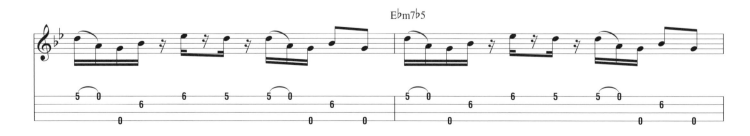

C

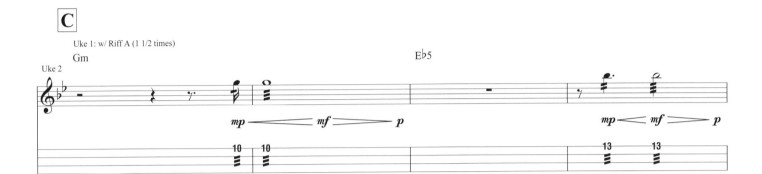

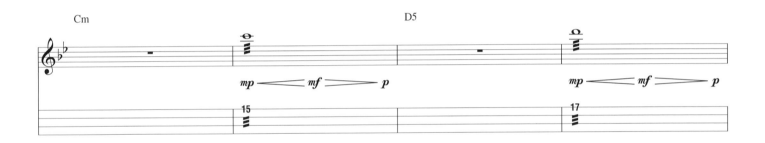

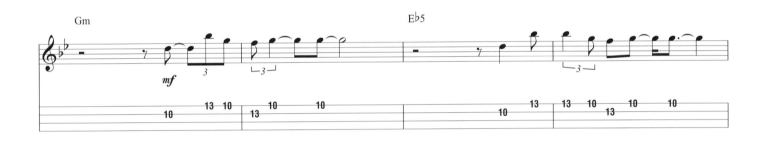

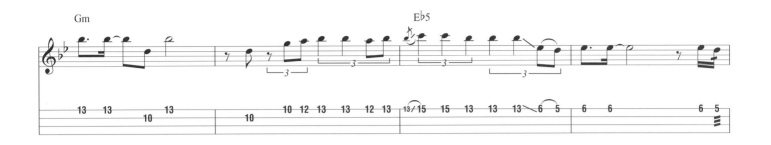

G

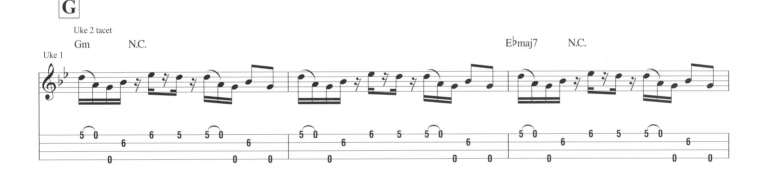

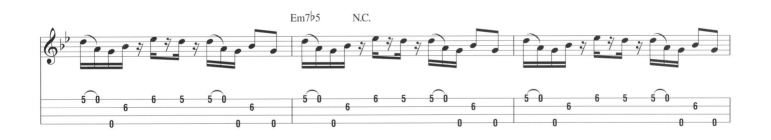

Morning Blue

Written by Jake Shimabukuro, Nolan Verner and David Preston Amidei

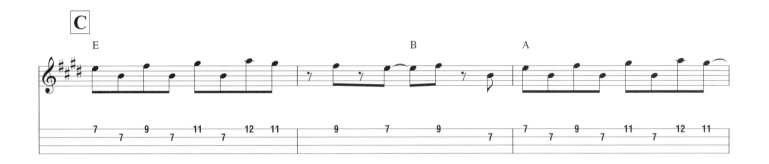

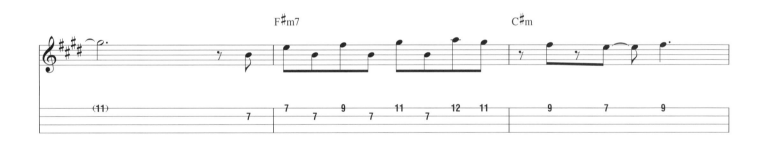

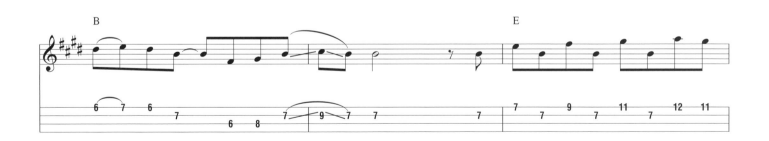

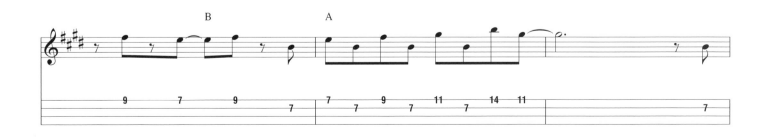

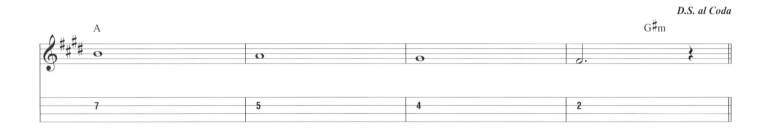

Coda

D

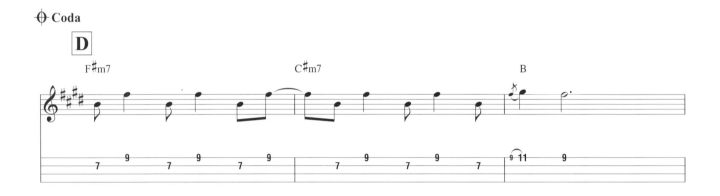

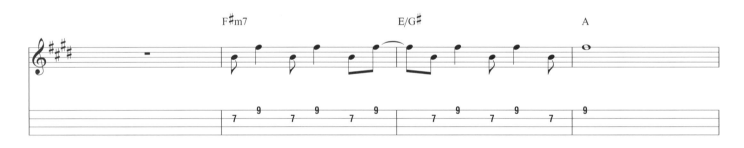

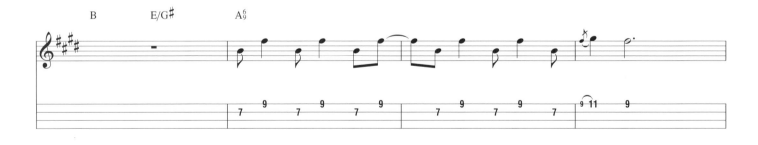

Summer Rain

Written by Jake Shimabukuro, Nolan Verner and David Preston Amidei

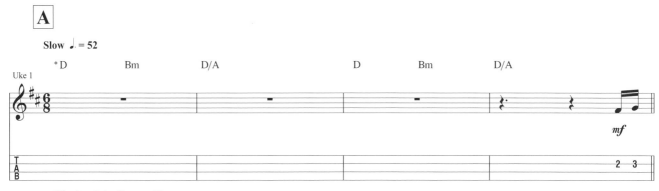

*Chord symbols reflect overall harmony.

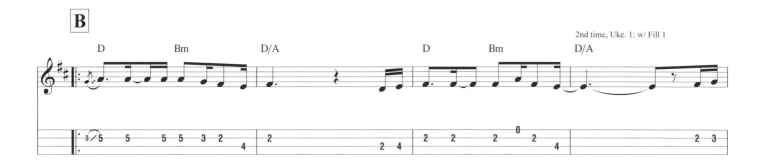

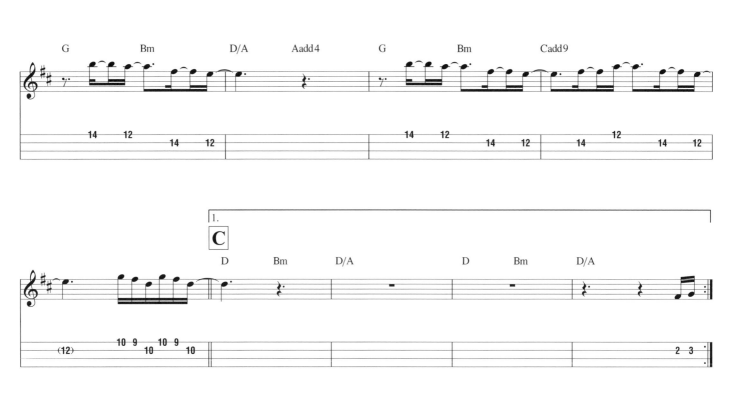

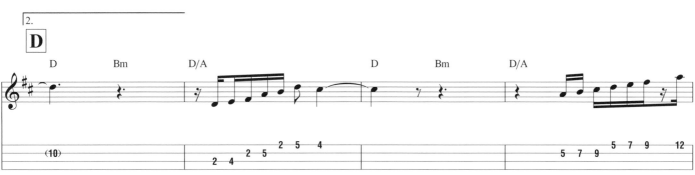

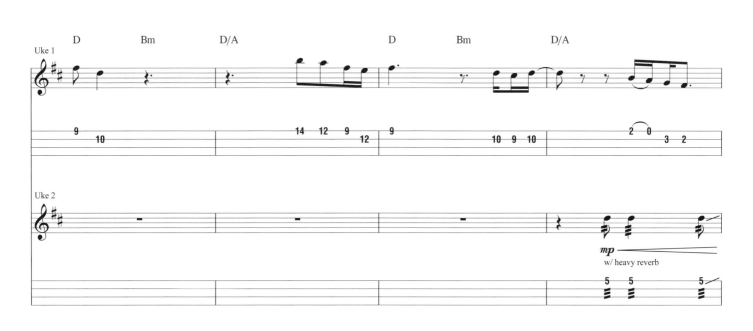

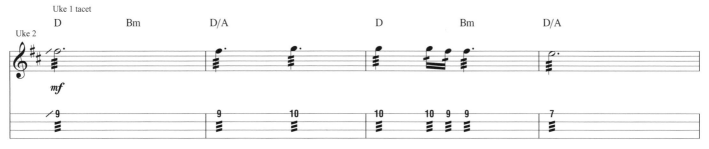

Wish You Were Here

Words and Music by Roger Waters and David Gilmour

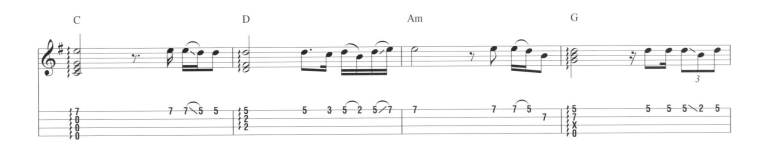

D

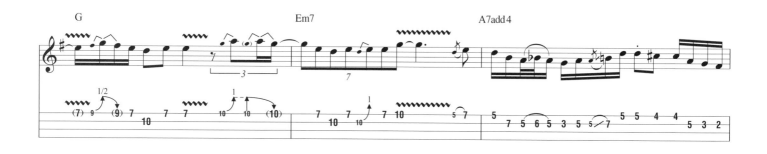

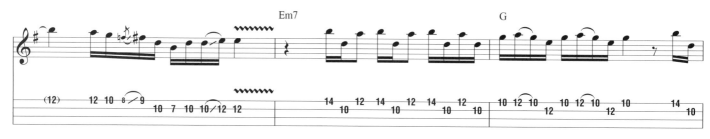

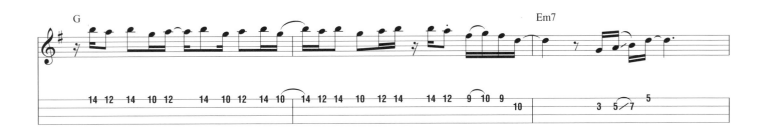

Free time

Fireflies

Written by Coleman Bear Saunders

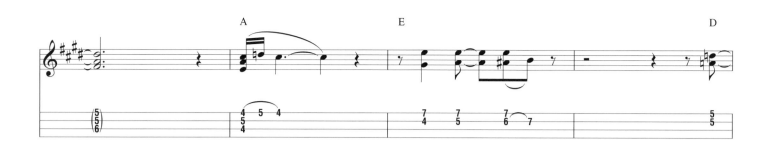

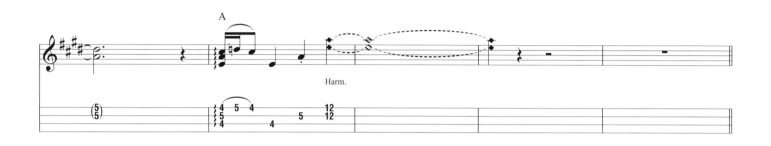

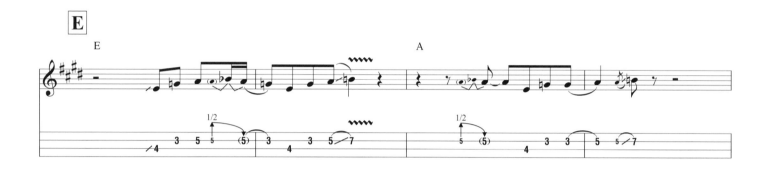

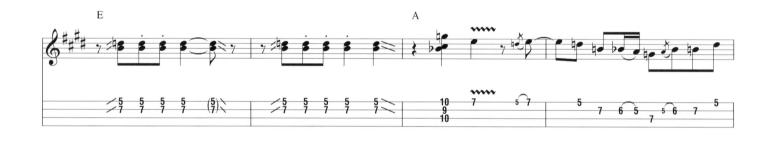

Begin fade

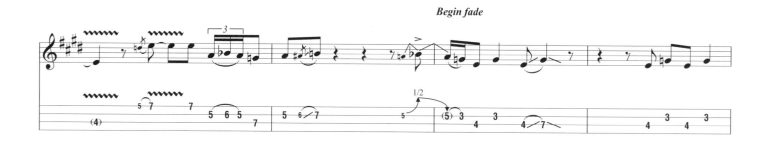

Fade out

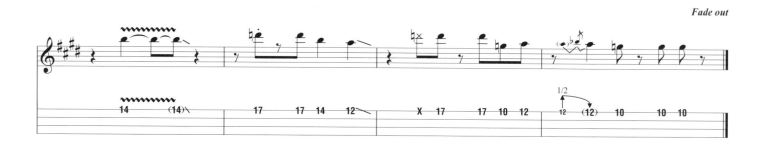

Wai'alae

Traditional Hawaiian Song
Arranged by Jake Shimabukuro

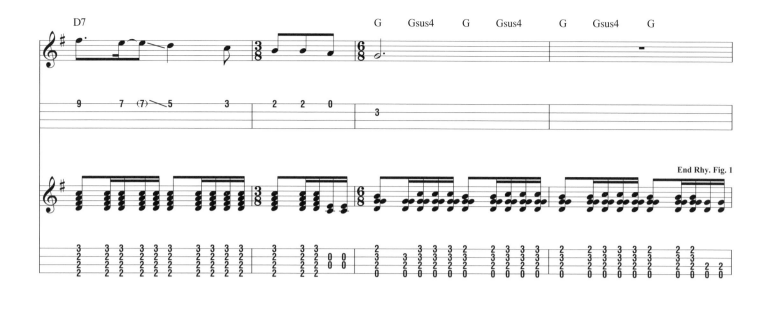

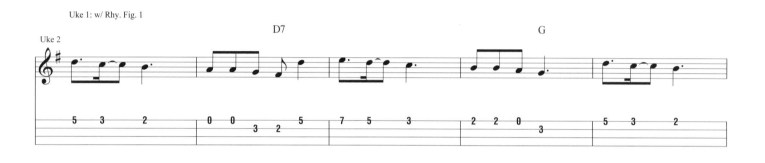

Uke 1: w/ Rhy. Fig. 1

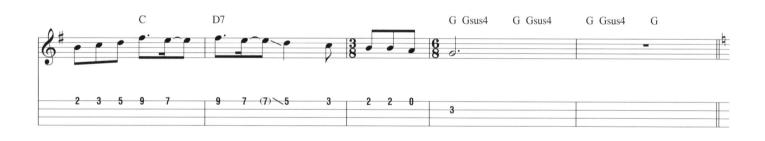

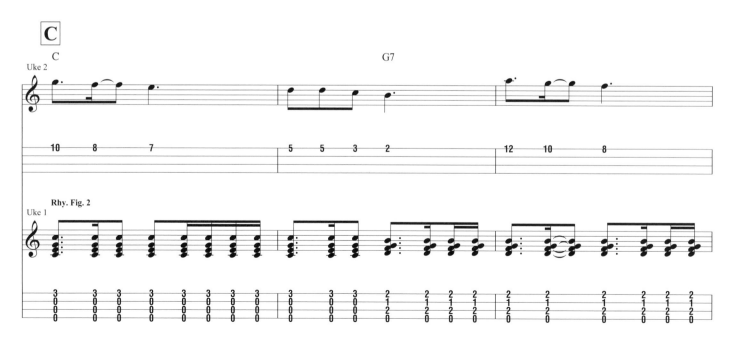

On the Wing

Written by Jake Shimabukuro, Nolan Verner and David Preston Amidei

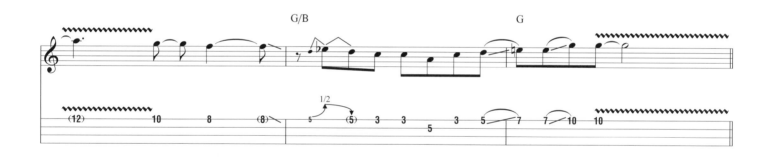

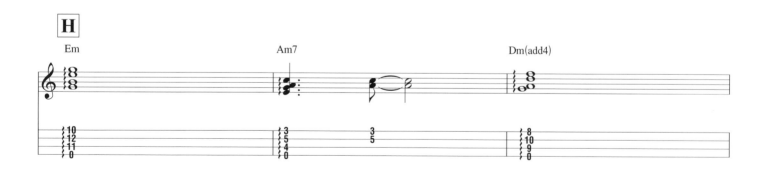

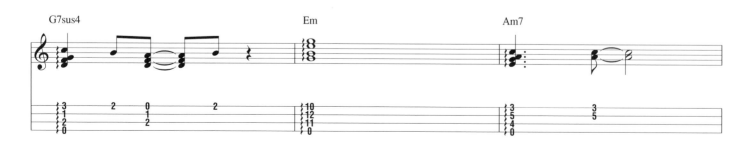

Strong in Broken Places

Written by Jake Shimabukuro, Nolan Verner and David Preston Amidei

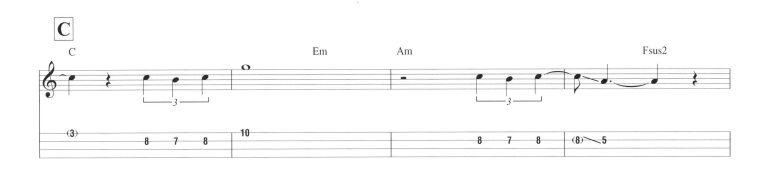

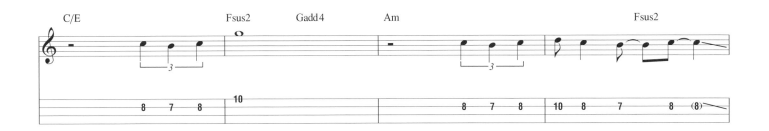

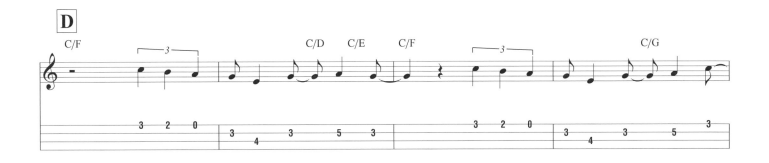

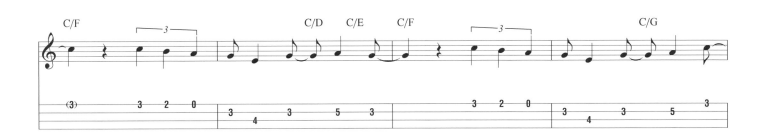

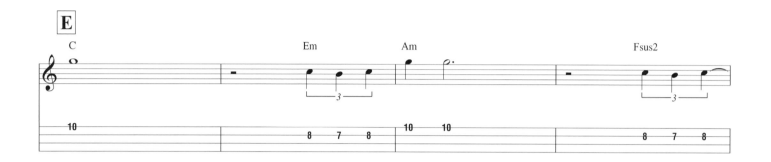

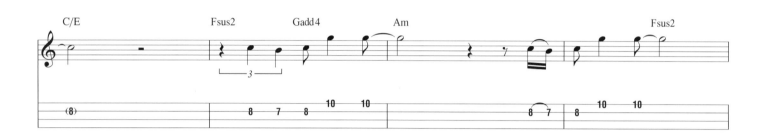

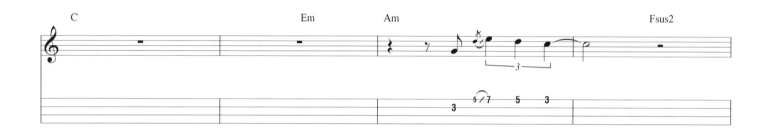

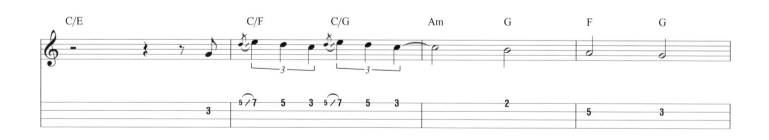

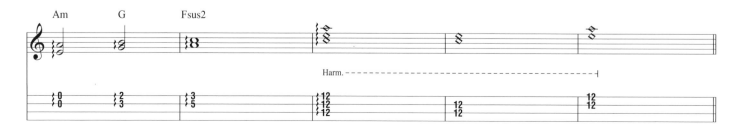

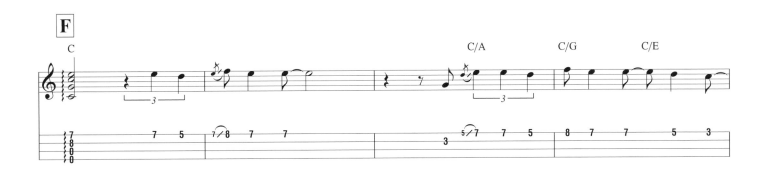

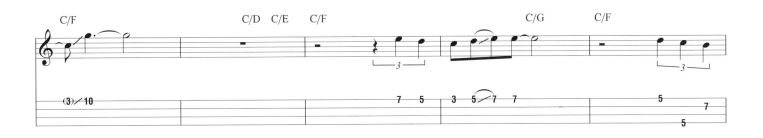

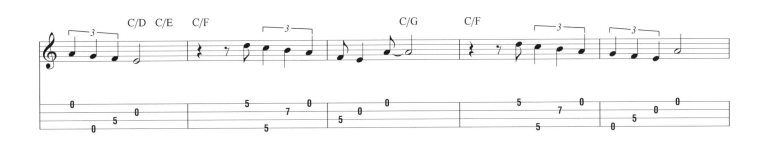

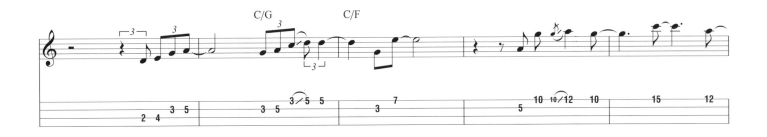

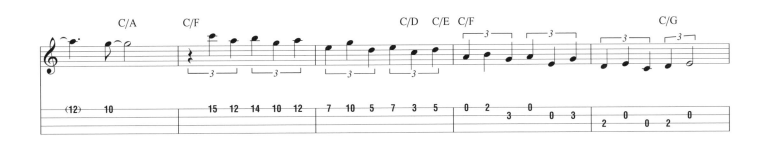

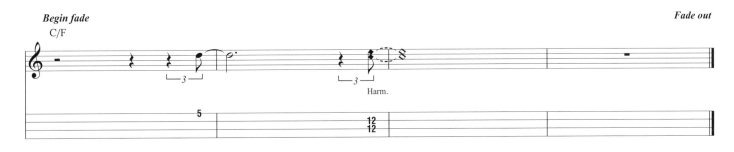

Landslide

Words and Music by Stevie Nicks

Intro
Moderately slow ♩ = 75

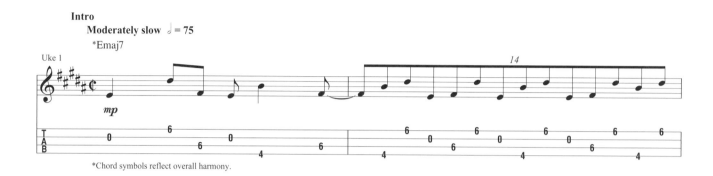

*Chord symbols reflect overall harmony.

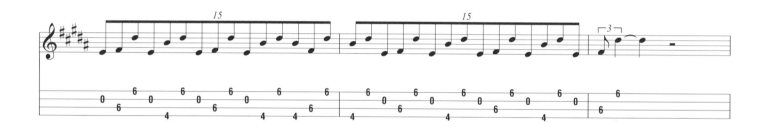

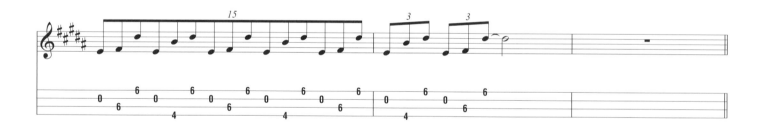

Verse

1. Took my love, ___ and I took it down. ___

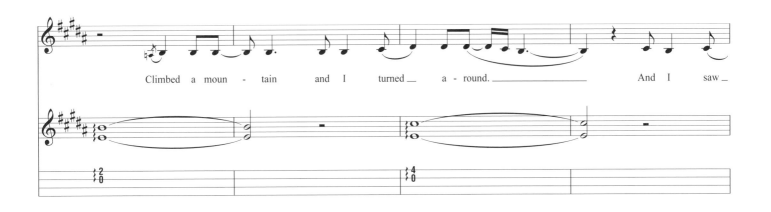

Climbed a moun - tain and I turned _ a - round. _____ And I saw _

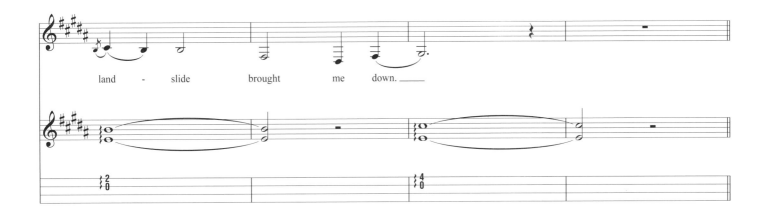

_ my _ re - flec - tion in the snow _ cov - ered hills _____ where the

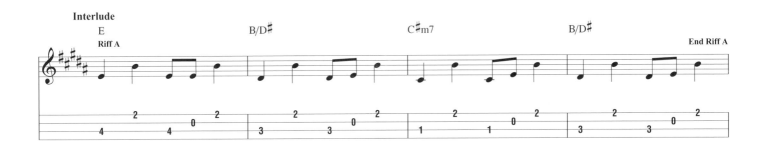

land - slide brought me down. _____

Interlude

E   B/D#   C#m7   B/D#

Riff A   **End Riff A**

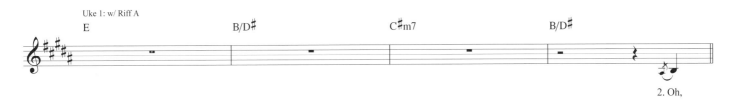

Uke 1: w/ Riff A

E   B/D#   C#m7   B/D#

2. Oh,

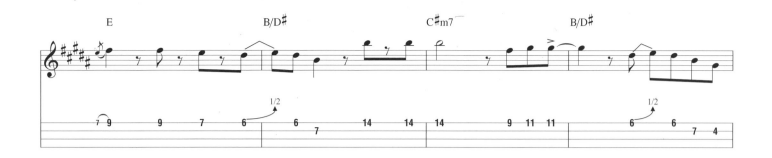

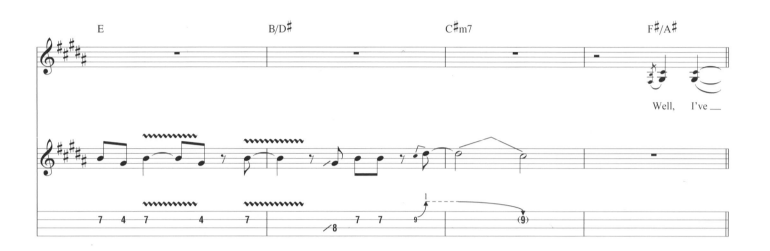

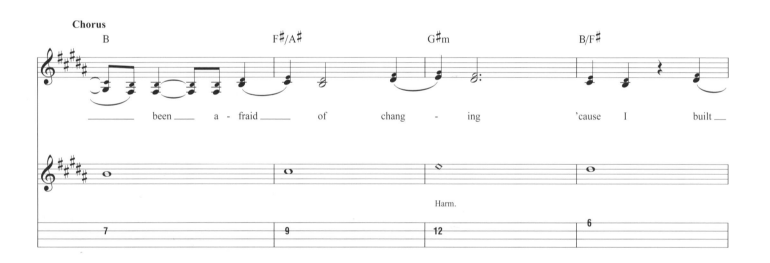

Chorus

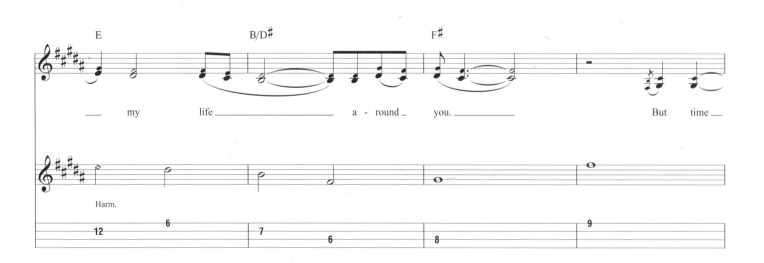

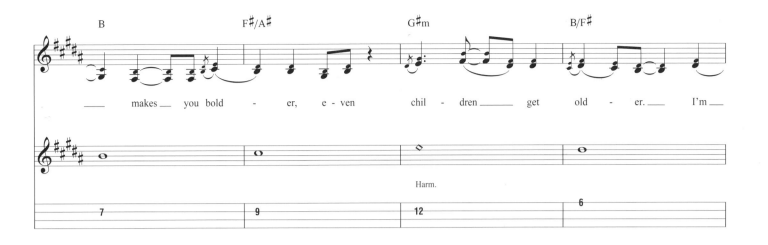

makes ___ you bold - er, e - ven chil - dren ___ get old - er. ___ I'm ___

___ get - ting old - er, too. ___

Outro

Uke 1: w/ Riff C (6 times)

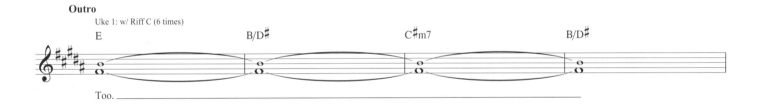

Too. ___

Too. ___

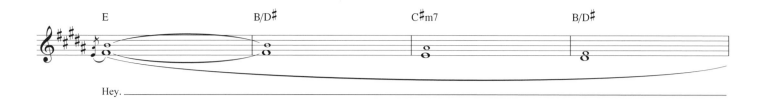

Hey.

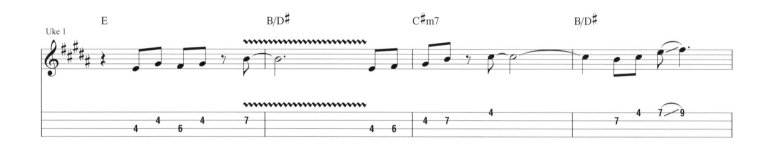

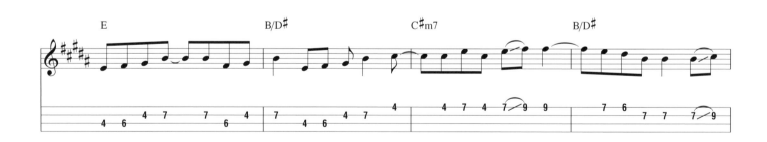

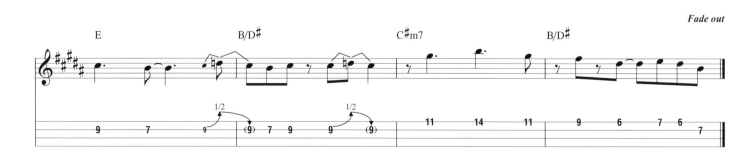

UKULELE NOTATION LEGEND

THE MUSICAL STAFF shows pitches and rhythms and is divided by bar lines into measures. Pitches are named after the first seven letters of the alphabet.

TABLATURE graphically represents the ukulele fingerboard. Each horizontal line represents a a string, and each number represents a fret.

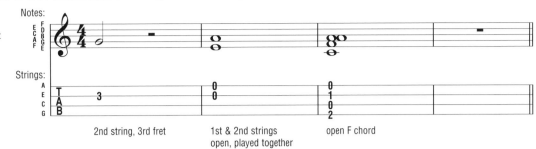

2nd string, 3rd fret

1st & 2nd strings open, played together

open F chord

HALF-STEP BEND: Strike the note and bend up 1/2 step.

WHOLE-STEP BEND: Strike the note and bend up one step.

GRACE NOTE BEND: Strike the note and immediately bend up as indicated.

SLIGHT (MICROTONE) BEND: Strike the note and bend up 1/4 step.

BEND AND RELEASE: Strike the note and bend up as indicated, then release back to the original note. Only the first note is struck.

PRE-BEND: Bend the note as indicated, then strike it.

VIBRATO: The string is vibrated by rapidly bending and releasing the note with the fretting hand.

HAMMER-ON: Strike the first (lower) note with one finger, then sound the higher note (on the same string) with another finger by fretting it without picking.

PULL-OFF: Place both fingers on the notes to be sounded. Strike the first note and without picking, pull the finger off to sound the second (lower) note.

LEGATO SLIDE: Strike the first note and then slide the same fret-hand finger up or down to the second note. The second note is not struck.

SHIFT SLIDE: Same as legato slide, except the second note is struck.

TRILL: Very rapidly alternate between the notes indicated by continuously hammering on and pulling off.

TREMOLO PICKING: The note is picked as rapidly and continuously as possible.

NOTE: Tablature numbers in parentheses mean:

1. The note is being sustained over a system (note in standard notation is tied), or

2. The note is sustained, but a new articulation (such as a hammer-on, pull-off, slide or vibrato) begins, or

3. The note is a barely audible "ghost" note (note in standard notation is also in parentheses).

Additional Musical Definitions

(accent)

- Accentuate note (play it louder)

(staccato)

- Play the note short

D.S. al Coda

- Go back to the sign (%), then play until the measure marked "*To Coda*," then skip to the section labelled "**Coda**."

D.C. al Fine

- Go back to the beginning of the song and play until the measure marked "*Fine*" (end).

N.C.

- No chord.

- Repeat measures between signs.

- When a repeated section has different endings, play the first ending only the first time and the second ending only the second time.

Ride the Ukulele Wave!

The Beach Boys for Ukulele

This folio features 20 favorites, including: Barbara Ann • Be True to Your School • California Girls • Fun, Fun, Fun • God Only Knows • Good Vibrations • Help Me Rhonda • I Get Around • In My Room • Kokomo • Little Deuce Coupe • Sloop John B • Surfin' U.S.A. • Wouldn't It Be Nice • and more!

00701726 . . . . $14.99

Disney Songs for Ukulele

20 great Disney classics arranged for all uke players, including: Beauty and the Beast • Bibbidi-Bobbidi-Boo (The Magic Song) • Can You Feel the Love Tonight • Chim Chim Cher-ee • Heigh-Ho • It's a Small World • Some Day My Prince Will Come • We're All in This Together • When You Wish upon a Star • and more.

00701708 . . . . $14.99

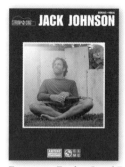

Jack Johnson – Strum & Sing

Cherry Lane Music
Strum along with 41 Jack Johnson songs using this top-notch collection of chords and lyrics just for the uke! Includes: Better Together • Bubble Toes • Cocoon • Do You Remember • Flake • Fortunate Fool • Good People • Holes to Heaven • Taylor • Tomorrow Morning • and more.

02501702 . . . . $19.99

The Beatles for Ukulele

Ukulele players can strum, sing and pick along with 20 Beatles classics! Includes: All You Need Is Love • Eight Days a Week • Good Day Sunshine • Here, There and Everywhere • Let It Be • Love Me Do • Penny Lane • Yesterday • and more.

00700154 . . . . $16.99

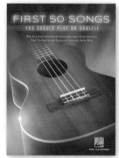

First 50 Songs You Should Play on Ukulele

An amazing collection of 50 accessible, must-know favorites: Edelweiss • Hey, Soul Sister • I Walk the Line • I'm Yours • Imagine • Over the Rainbow • Peaceful Easy Feeling • The Rainbow Connection • Riptide • and many more.

00149250 . . . . $14.99

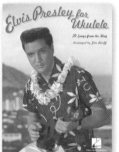

Elvis Presley for Ukulele

arr. Jim Beloff
20 classic hits from The King: All Shook Up • Blue Hawaii • Blue Suede Shoes • Can't Help Falling in Love • Don't • Heartbreak Hotel • Hound Dog • Jailhouse Rock • Love Me • Love Me Tender • Return to Sender • Suspicious Minds • Teddy Bear • and more.

00701004 . . . . $15.99

The Daily Ukulele

compiled and arranged by
Liz and Jim Beloff
Strum a different song everyday with easy arrangements of 365 of your favorite songs in one big songbook! Includes favorites by the Beatles, Beach Boys, and Bob Dylan, folk songs, pop songs, kids' songs, Christmas carols, and Broadway and Hollywood tunes, all with a spiral binding for ease of use.

00240356 . . . . $39.99

Folk Songs for Ukulele

A great collection to take along to the campfire! 60 folk songs, including: Amazing Grace • Buffalo Gals • Camptown Races • For He's a Jolly Good Fellow • Good Night Ladies • Home on the Range • I've Been Working on the Railroad • Kumbaya • My Bonnie Lies over the Ocean • On Top of Old Smoky • Scarborough Fair • Swing Low, Sweet Chariot • Take Me Out to the Ball Game • Yankee Doodle • and more.

00696068 . . . . $12.99

Jake Shimabukuro – Peace Love Ukulele

Deemed "the Hendrix of the ukulele," Hawaii native Jake Shimabukuro is a uke virtuoso. Our songbook features note-for-note transcriptions with ukulele tablature of Jake's masterful playing on all the CD tracks: Bohemian Rhapsody • Boy Meets Girl • Bring Your Adz • Hallelujah • Pianoforte 2010 • Variation on a Dance 2010 • and more, plus two bonus selections!

00702516 . . . . $19.99

The Daily Ukulele – Leap Year Edition

366 More Songs for Better Living
compiled and arranged by
Liz and Jim Beloff
An amazing second volume with 366 MORE songs for you to master each day of a leap year! Includes: Ain't No Sunshine • Calendar Girl • I Got You Babe • Lean on Me • Moondance • and many, many more.

00240681 . . . . $39.99

Hawaiian Songs for Ukulele

Over thirty songs from the state that made the ukulele famous, including: Beyond the Rainbow • Hanalei Moon • Ka-lu-a • Lovely Hula Girl • Mele Kalikimaka • One More Aloha • Sea Breeze • Tiny Bubbles • Waikiki • and more.

00696065 . . . . $10.99

Worship Songs for Ukulele

25 worship songs: Amazing Grace (My Chains are Gone) • Blessed Be Your Name • Enough • God of Wonders • Holy Is the Lord • How Great Is Our God • In Christ Alone • Love the Lord • Mighty to Save • Sing to the King • Step by Step • We Fall Down • and more.

00702546 . . . . $14.99

Disney characters and artwork © Disney Enterprises, Inc.

HAL•LEONARD®

Prices, contents, and availability subject to change.

0119
479

HAL·LEONARD® UKULELE PLAY-ALONG

AUDIO ACCESS INCLUDED

1. POP HITS
00701451 Book/CD Pack..............$15.99

2. UKE CLASSICS
00701452 Book/CD Pack..............$15.99

3. HAWAIIAN FAVORITES
00701453 Book/Online Audio.........$14.99

4. CHILDREN'S SONGS
00701454 Book/Online Audio.........$14.99

5. CHRISTMAS SONGS
00701696 Book/CD Pack..............$12.99

6. LENNON & MCCARTNEY
00701723 Book/Online Audio.........$12.99

7. DISNEY FAVORITES
00701724 Book/Online Audio.........$12.99

8. CHART HITS
00701745 Book/CD Pack..............$15.99

9. THE SOUND OF MUSIC
00701784 Book/CD Pack..............$14.99

10. MOTOWN
00701964 Book/CD Pack..............$12.99

11. CHRISTMAS STRUMMING
00702458 Book/Online Audio.........$12.99

12. BLUEGRASS FAVORITES
00702584 Book/CD Pack..............$12.99

13. UKULELE SONGS
00702599 Book/CD Pack..............$12.99

14. JOHNNY CASH
00702615 Book/CD Pack..............$15.99

15. COUNTRY CLASSICS
00702834 Book/CD Pack..............$12.99

16. STANDARDS
00702835 Book/CD Pack..............$12.99

17. POP STANDARDS
00702836 Book/CD Pack..............$12.99

18. IRISH SONGS
00703086 Book/Online Audio.........$12.99

19. BLUES STANDARDS
00703087 Book/CD Pack..............$12.99

20. FOLK POP ROCK
00703088 Book/CD Pack..............$12.99

21. HAWAIIAN CLASSICS
00703097 Book/CD Pack..............$12.99

22. ISLAND SONGS
00703098 Book/CD Pack..............$12.99

23. TAYLOR SWIFT – 2ND EDITION
00221966 Book/Online Audio.........$16.99

24. WINTER WONDERLAND
00101871 Book/CD Pack..............$12.99

25. GREEN DAY
00110398 Book/CD Pack..............$14.99

26. BOB MARLEY
00110399 Book/Online Audio.........$14.99

27. TIN PAN ALLEY
00116358 Book/CD Pack..............$12.99

28. STEVIE WONDER
00116736 Book/CD Pack..............$14.99

29. OVER THE RAINBOW & OTHER FAVORITES
00117076 Book/Online Audio.........$14.99

30. ACOUSTIC SONGS
00122336 Book/CD Pack..............$14.99

31. JASON MRAZ
00124166 Book/CD Pack..............$14.99

32. TOP DOWNLOADS
00127507 Book/CD Pack..............$14.99

33. CLASSICAL THEMES
00127892 Book/Online Audio.........$14.99

34. CHRISTMAS HITS
00128602 Book/CD Pack..............$14.99

35. SONGS FOR BEGINNERS
00129009 Book/Online Audio.........$14.99

36. ELVIS PRESLEY HAWAII
00138199 Book/Online Audio.........$14.99

37. LATIN
00141191 Book/Online Audio.........$14.99

38. JAZZ
00141192 Book/Online Audio.........$14.99

39. GYPSY JAZZ
00146559 Book/Online Audio.........$14.99

40. TODAY'S HITS
00160845 Book/Online Audio.........$14.99

Prices, contents, and availability subject to change without notice.

HAL·LEONARD®

www.halleonard.com